This is a book to help ease some of those questions that you might have about you or your loved one going to jail for the first time. We all say, "That will never happen to me or my family!" But we truly never know what may happen in the future so I came up with this book as a help or guidance guide for when the unexpected happens.

I don't know how many times in jail or prison you will hear someone say it wasn't their fault or they never meant to hurt anyone! Just because someone has been in jail or prison does not make them a bad person. Bad things happen to good people all the time. Maybe they had a new or inexperienced public defender because they could not afford a good attorney. Maybe they were set up by someone who was supposed to care and love them or maybe bad cops?

This has always been the saying in this house: "Never judge anyone until you have walked a mile in their shoes!" And as we all know most of us will never walk in someone else's shoes so just don't judge people.

If there had been a book like this around when my family and I had to go though our ordeal with incarceration, we would have definitely used it and passed it around for sure. So with that said I hope this helps you and your loved ones help make a bad situation a little understandable and somewhat ease your minds.

Doing Time

The first piece of good advice I will give you will be: do not do anything that might put you in a situation that might make you face some incarceration. But we all say I will never go to jail or do that. It does happen to the best of people though.

I knew a 17 year old girl who went out with two of her friends late one night to just go grab a bite to eat after a football game. Their parents said ok and be safe. This girl had never been in trouble and was well liked by many of her peers. As they were leaving the dinner to go back home she hit a patch of gravel and slid over an embankment. She was almost killed had her arm severed and actually died two times on the way to the hospital to have surgery. When she came to after surgery she asked about her two best friends and her parents had to tell her the awful truth. Both her best friends had died on impact in the crash and then had to tell her she would never fully be able to use her right arm again.

This young girl turned 18 right before they had her trail for the deaths of her friends. The court tried her as an adult and she now has to do 10 years for the unintentional death of the two best friends she loved dearly.

I used this one story just to prove a point that she was not doing anything wrong or breaking any law. She never wanted to kill her friends and was a good student, friend, sister, and family member. This young lady will now have the title of convicted felon and will have an even harder road ahead of her when she is eventually released from prison when she is 28 years old.

I am not saying that she should not have to pay for the two young lives that is now lost. She will forever have to deal with the deaths of those two friends. I just think that it is so wrong that if you hurt a child or kill a baby intentionally they might get a few years but if it was an honest accident it should be looked at differently. This is just my opinion and a little story I wanted to share so you can open your eyes just a little as to why I have put all this together. Every time you or your loved one gets behind the wheel, you or them could unintentionally kill another motorist and face a stiff prison time. That is where this guide comes in.

Prepare Yourself

If you are facing some jail time prepare yourself and your loved ones for this absence in their lives. It is hard enough for your loved ones to have to make it while you are not around for months or years. If you are one of the luck few that have a loving and caring family, that will add the extra added stress of sending you money to help buy everyday personal hygiene products. The cost of everything in jail is almost triple what we would pay out on the street.

If you are among the lucky few that get to turn yourself in at a later date after your sentencing, this short amount of time gives you time to share precious memories with loved ones and get yourself prepared for your incarceration.

No one ever wants to go to jail. But sometimes we have to do what we have to do. I am not going to lie and say at first I thought about running like so many people have before me. But I have two precious little girls and a caring and loving family/support system I could not leave behind. I know people who have tried suicide and some have failed and some have succeeded in doing so just because they are facing some time behind bars. Suicide is a permanent solution to a temporary problem.

Most people who are even thinking about suicide as a solution to their problems are just afraid of the future. Like those who are facing jail time for the first time and get to turn their selves in after sentencing. It will be ok! Jail is by no means a good place or great to be in but it is not as bad as the movies make it look. This book will teach you what to look forward to and expect in jail/prison. Think about it this way just do your time and then when you get out it will all be behind you and you will be able to move on in life with your loved ones. It really is not as bad as you might think!

Day 1

No matter if you got days or years, everyone will have to go to jail first before you go to prison later on.

Your first day they will take you back to a "holding area" called "booking." In booking you have your picture taken, forms will have to be filled out, and you will change your "street" clothes for your new jail clothes.

Some good advice for those of you who get to turn yourselves into jail, wear stretchy clothes and something comfortable. The reason behind this is most people will gain weight while incarcerated and if you came in with comfortable/stretchy clothes more than likely they will fit when you get to leave.

The form you have to fill out and questions asked will be things like: name, birth date, address, time to serve, charges, height, weight.

The picture that they take of you will be on your identification bracelet or card that you must keep on you at all times while incarcerated. So some good advice is to make it a good one because it will be seen by people everywhere.

If you have a decent booking officer, they will try to give you the run down on the major do's and do not's of jail. This is always helpful so that you do not get a "charge." I will explain this in more detail a little later. But the short version of getting a charge is like getting a ticket on the street. They will also tell you when you will have your meals and shower times.

Classifications

When some people go in they will be classified as a "protected custody" inmate. This means that you need to be watched a little closer so that other inmates do not cause you any harm or maybe you do not harm the other inmates with you. If you have ever been an officer or maybe worked in a jail/prison this classification is for your protection. If you are classified as a "P.C." inmate your time is going to be a little harder than some of the other inmates because of where you will be housed.

"Housing" or classification will be the following in a jail/prison: minimum, medium, maximum, or segregation security.

Minimum security means that you will have the most freedom inside the institution. This class of inmates gets to be on "work release" in some cases. "Work release" is when you came into jail fully sentenced and had a job on the outside, the judge and institution will allow you to continue to go to work so you can keep your job. Someone has to pick you up from jail and drop you off for your work or the jail runs vans that will do the same but they charge you $15 a day to do it. They drug test you before they let you do work release and will do many random testing as well to make sure you are following the rules of the institution. If you fail any test you lose your job and get sent to the "jail inside jail" called maximum security for awhile, also called "lock down."

Minimum security also is an open pod with a lot of inmates all together. You have to share everything. There is only one shower, toilet, mirror, and sink. All the beds are metal bunk beds in this pod.

Medium security is in my opinion the best option out of the three. In this pod you have cells with two beds bolted to the walls, meant to look like bunk beds. Each cell has its own toilet, sink, and mirror. Out in the common area it also has one shower, toilet, sink, mirror, a "duck pond," metal bolted down tables, two phones, and a television on the side of the wall.

A duck pond is a small area on the floor next to the wall that has approximately 3 inch walls all in the shape of a box with a drain in the center. Up above this area will be a long hose and a hot water and cold water button. In the pods people will use these to get hot water for soups, coffee.

In this pod you can come in and out of your cell almost anytime you want with a few exceptions. You can come out at 6am and you have to go up when the officers do count before lunch and at dinner then you must go back in your cell at night at 10:30pm. At 10:30pm the lights go out or well they get very dim so you can sleep at night.

In maximum security pods you have the same things as medium security except you are now going to be locked up for 22 hours a day. You will still have a cell with no more than one person in it with you. It is stricter in this pod than minimum.

If you ever get put in this classification because you got into trouble inside the jail you will be on "lock down." Which means you cannot use the phones or watch any television during this lock down time and you can only come out of your cell for one hour each day too.

You have to eat all your meals inside your cell and the only jobs you can have in this pod are: pod cleaner or tray sever. Pod cleaners get out every other day to clean the entire pod from top to bottom. Tray servers get out three times extra a day to pass out the trays that they give to inmates and then have to go collect them back up. You as a tray sever are responsible for all the trays, cups, and sporks that come with each meal. Before you are allowed to go back to your cell after each meal, the officers must count each tray, cup, and sporks to make sure they are accounted for. If the count is off let's say a sporks is missing, the tray servers have around 2 minutes to collect the sporks from whoever kept it or the whole pod will be shook down until they find it! "Shook down" means the officers will search everything in that pod from you and your clothes to the toilets in each cell.

Some people like to stay in max because you do not have to deal with all the other inmates and you have your own toilet. It is for the most part quiet and if you cannot stand being by yourself this is not the pod for you. Sometimes if you are in this pod you will have the whole cell to yourself, which is nice. But like I said earlier if you cannot stand being by yourself with no one to talk to for 22 hours a day you will want to stay away from max.

Segregation is the same setup as max but it is usually reserved for the protective custody inmates or those who have to be kept away from other inmates for medical reasons.

Rules of the Pods

There are some rules that will not be listed in the institution rule book for inmates to follow. What I mean by this is that inmates have a set of their own understood rules to help things run a little better during your stay in the pods.

You need to set all of your shower things next to the shower or call out your after so and so when they get out of the shower so you will be next in line. The phone use is the same way. There are only two phones that look like a pay phone on the side of one wall. Call out or tell the person who is using the phone at the time you are to be next to use the phone. The phone calls can only last 15 minutes at a time then they automatically cut off then you have to either get back in line or if no one is waiting you can use the phone again.

You must get your own tray unless it is a special circumstance, like being in max or very sick.

Never talk about how much time you have to other inmates unless they personally ask you. The reason behind this is some people have years to serve or maybe even life. If you go around talking about how you cannot do 30 days and cry about your time, you will piss off the other inmates who have some serious time to pull. Everyone has a family or maybe even kids they did not want to leave to come to jail to do their time. So no one wants to hear how you have to do 2 weeks and you have never left your kids alone. So for these reasons right here do not go around telling other inmates how much time you have if they did not ask you first.

Do not go around crying, if you can help it. It makes your time and others time with you much harder than it needs to be. Like I said earlier, we all have loved ones who we had to leave to do our time. I am not saying that we all don't cry every once in awhile but when you do the other inmates will usually try to help you get through it by talking to you or try to take your mind off of your issues.

If you have people you write often, never leave their address out where other inmates can see them and possibly write down the address. Some people just like to start trouble and if they see that you are writing someone often and in turn they are keeping money on your account to spend, they will try to write them too. So what you will learn is to get a bible and on the back page of your bible write down all the phone numbers and address of the people you write or know for safe keeping. A lot of people will even go so far as to rip up the letters and envelopes and flush or throw them away when they finish reading them. This is a big rule especially in the open pod or minimum security pod.

Do not trust anybody! It does not matter who they are. They could have been your best friend out on the street. If you have a secret, do not tell a soul because the first time your buddy gets pissed off at you, they will tell. Snitches are everywhere in jail. People who never snitched on the street will turn in jail and we never really know why you would wait until you're in jail to do this but it does happen a lot! A "snitch" or a "rat" is a person who tells on others for some kind of personal gain who works for police of any kind including corrections officers inside of jail.

If you "buy" or "borough" something from another inmate, you better make sure you pay for it or give back what you are suppose too. If you fail to do so and try to cheat them out of it, they can and will beat it out of you. It will be painful for you and they will just get to go to max for a little while, if they are even caught. My best advice for this is try not to do either of the above but if you do promise something to another inmate for something you received from them, just pay it back!

The crimes that no inmates will tolerate in jail are: crimes committed against children and the elderly. By crimes against children I mean: any type of rape, murder, abuse, neglect. By crimes against the elderly I mean beating on them, abuse, neglect, robbing. Most inmates that come into the jail with any of these types of crimes against them will automatically go into the protective custody section or max side of the jail. If they ever do get around any other inmates most of the time the other inmates will beat them or torture them to the point of having to go to the hospital! So all the child molesters and murderers will always get what they deserve for the innocent lives they forever ruined.

Commissary

This will be one word you will know all about within about a week and love it! Even if you do not have people who can put money on your "books" or your account, you can still order from the commissary.

An easy way to think about commissary is like a grocery store. If you are indigent, which means you have no money at all on your books. You can order an indigent pack every week but the down side to this is it charges your account $5 each time you order one of these packs. So if you have someone put money on your account later on, it always deducts your past due balance on your commissary account first! So if this happens and you have a lot of money you owe for the packs you had been ordering. Have a close buddy that you trust that will let you order on their account so you can get your stuff. This is however against the institution rules to order things for another inmate but sometimes you have to do what you have to do. Have your people place your money on your buddies account for you then you can order the things you need like toothpaste or deodorant.

This is how you can order from commissary. There are two ways to order from commissary while incarcerated. The first one is by a paper form and the second one is by an electronic form on a "kiosk." A kiosk is a touch screen computer that allows inmates to communicate with the mental health counselors, medical staff, and officers quickly and gives the inmate a receipt to show if needed about a matter. On the kiosk you will find a button for commissary that will allow you to order everything you might need and also show you how much money you have to spend on commissary items for that week. The limit you can spend each week on commissary items is currently $75. Now a lot of people will say $75 is way more than I spend each week on the outside, or that is way too much to spend inside of jail for a week! Well that is exactly why I have written this book to explain things like this to the public. On the inside the prices of things are almost triple if not more on what we call everyday products like deodorant or toothpaste. When you first come into jail most of your first order will be nothing but the basics you need to have in jail. Some of those things are: a cup with a lid, a bowl with a lid, deodorant, toothpaste, hair comb, at least one pair of boxers (for both men and women), 5 envelopes, 5 pieces of paper, ink pen, pencil, a bar of soap and a soap dish to put it in, shampoo, conditioner (if needed), a spoon, and then some food. Examples of some prices are: $3 for a small bottle of Vo5 shampoo when in the stores you can get the same bottle sometimes even bigger for $0.98! Deodorant and toothpaste are the same story, Degree deodorant is sold in jail for $3.50 when you can buy it in the dollar tree for $1. At the end of this book I will try to put in photo copies so some of the commissary receipt forms that I kept just to show you all the crazy prices of items that we have to have. The items that they give you in the indigent packs I will explain in better detail and what you can use them for because the items that come in it are not good for what they say to use it for. And just a little FYI when you walk into jail you automatically get charged $5 for an indigent pack even if you never get it because: you bail out or they forgot to give it to you in booking! So something good to do if you ever get put in booking, give your packet to someone in there that looks like they could use the extra items. You don't have to give them away because if you really wanted to you could take it out with you, after all you did pay for it! But really what is the point in doing that?!

There are other things on the commissary list for purchase too. You cannot buy any type of razor on commissary. The state issues each inmate one razor to be used within a short amount of time then it has to be inspected and turned into the officer that gave you the razor to begin with.

Working

When you are in jail you can apply for jobs that are available in your pod. If you do get a job in jail you cannot earn any money for you to use, it is only to pay off fines. For example if you have a $500 fine from court, you can work it off in the kitchen at $8/hour until your fine is paid off in full. After the fine is paid off the rest of the time you work in the kitchen is like community service. You never get paid any money to keep or use to buy things in the commissary. A lot of inmates come in thinking that you can work and make a little money to buy things in commissary you need like toothpaste or shampoo but you cannot do that in jail. In prison you can work and earn money but you only get paid $1 or less an hour instead of minimum wage. If you ever have the option of going to jail or prison anyone you talk to that has done both will tell you prison is a lot easier to do time in. I will talk a little more about the differences toward the end of the book.

In most jails there will be a "kitchen" pod. In this pod they will try to keep only the kitchen workers. A lot of inmates try to get in this pod for a lot reasons. If you work in the kitchen you have the highest paying job for an inmate in the entire jail! You also get to eat a lot too. You will get the normal three meals a day plus you can eat some extra things as well. This is where a lot of inmates will gain weight. You cannot bring food back to your cell with you at the end of your work shift though. Some will try to sneak food back but if you are caught, you will be fired and will most likely never be able to work in the kitchen again and go to max for punishment. This pod is also a minimum housing unit as well, which means more freedom than the other two housing classifications. When you apply for the kitchen too you have to be medically cleared as well. This means that you are free and clear of all contagious diseases and sicknesses. This means you cannot have AIDS, Hepatitis, ect. So for those of you who think that eating in jail is nasty, think about this: Do you think that when you go eat at a restaurant in the public that every employee handling your food is free of any sickness or diseases that you could possibly catch?! It is the best and honest thing to do for those people with things such as Hepatitis, to not work with food that the public consumes but it does not always work out that way. Just a little something for you all to think about the next time you talk about how nasty jailhouse food is!

Here is a list of some of the other jobs that might be available in minimum pods.

Library workers, they get to go to the library Monday through Friday and help the librarian with anything they need done including passing out library books once a week.

Pod cleaners and tray servers. The pod cleaners get to clean each day unlike the other pods. The tray servers get to pass out the trays to all the other pods with the officers. In all the other pods except in max, the inmates get to walk up to the windows in each pod to get their own trays and give them back when they are done at each meal.

Laundry workers stay in this pod as well. Laundry workers get out every day to go to the laundry room.

If you had a job on the outside before jail and you get approved through court and the jail to continue to work at your job this is the pod you must stay in to keep your job. If you get into trouble and get moved to another pod, you lose your job. Unless you have a really understanding boss and you can call and explain why you cannot get to work now from jail and they keep your job for when you get released from jail. (This does not happen that often, most bosses will not keep your job for you.)

Courthouse workers. Usually just two people will be picked and maybe a backup for when one is sick or cannot go that day. They get to go to the courthouse Monday through Friday to clean.

Road trash crew. From march until around November the jail will pick around 8 to 10 people to go with an officer to pick up road trash a few days a week, only when the conditions outside are suitable to do so.

Outside hallway cleaners. These people clean the visitation areas, administration offices, hallways, and a few other areas each night.

If you are thinking about applying for any of the outside jobs, not inside of the jail or allow you to temporarily leave the jail facility. You must be "outside" approved. This means that you have to be fully sentenced, have no violent convictions, be charge free (stayed out of trouble inside jail) for a period of time, and have less than a year left to serve.

In medium security there are only two jobs just like max: pod cleaner and tray server. The only difference is that the pod cleaners clean every night and in max they only get to clean every other night. The tray servers get to pass trays to the other pods when the minimum pod does not.

The workers in maximum security pods never get to leave to do any work.

Also in Max any time you leave the pod no matter if it is to go to medical or even visitation you MUST be handcuffed before leaving the common area in the pod. It is for everyone else's safety inside of the jail. They consider the Max inmates to be the real bad guys of the institution!

Visitation Times

In jail the men and women have different times that the family can come visit them on the weekends only! The Max inmates are always first in the morning because there are usually fewer of them and they all have to be cuffed before going to visitation! The women have first half of Saturday then the men have the rest of Saturday and all day Sunday.

Each pod will have a set posted time for visitations each weekend. Once you are placed in a pod you can find out when your visit will be with your family.

In prison you can get visits on both days on the weekends and even on every state recognized holiday. So in this way you can see your loved ones at least two times a week or more instead of just one day like in jail. Also the visits in jail can only last for 15 minutes then you have to go back to your cell. In prison you can spend as long as you would like unless the visitations get busy then they try to cut them to about 2 hrs each day.

In jail you can have no personal contact with the visitors. You have to sit behind a glass wall with a phone on each side and talk through the phones to each other. In prison you can give them a quick hug and kiss at the beginning of each visit and can see them and talk face to face while they sit on one side of a divider and you on the other. The divider looks like a long metal table with a small 6 inch wall going up the middle of it so that you cannot pass things to the person in front of you. Also in jail you can buy any soda product or snack item that is available in the machines at the back of visitations for your incarcerated loved one. You must bring in a lot of quarters or one dollar bills for the machines. The visitor must go to the snack area and purchase the items for the inmate then take it back to the table allow the officer to inspect it for contraband and then the officer will hand it to the inmate. This only applies to prison visitation!

Reduced Time

In Virginia you have to serve 50% on your misdemeanor time and 85% on your felony time. You can get some time taken off of your misdemeanor time by taking classes to help better yourself like your G.E.D. With felony time you can only get around 5 days with one class which you can only take in minimum security. The felony class is called DRIVE which is to help with drug and substance dependence. These classes do not always take time off of your sentence but if you do what you need to and pass the classes, you can get out a few days early.

Jailhouse Cookbook

When you get in jail the first thing you will see or hear people talk about will be what they will be cooking or fixing to eat later. You will need noodles for almost anything that you fix in jail. Most of the time that is the first thing that people will order. If you have to have coffee but you do not get a lot of money it would be best to order coffee first then food. People love to make and eat "bricks" in institutions. A brick is a term used by inmates to describe a type of food that holds its shape and looks like a brick.

To make a brick you will need the following: a pack of noodles, a bag of chips, a pickle, tuna, hot water, and hot pretzel pieces. You have to crush the noodles, chips, and pretzel pieces. Cut the pickle up into little pieces to mix in later in the brick. I used my chip bag to mix and cook the ingredients when I finished, so try not to poke a hole in the bag. Add all the crushed ingredients in the chip bag with the seasoning packet from the noodles and shake to coat the bag. Add the pickle next then the tuna if you would like to add them. Shake again to mix well. Then add hot water to the bag, just enough to cover the ingredients. Roll down the top of the bag and mix well inside the bag. I always used tape or a hair bow to keep the top down on the bag and some even wrapped it in old newspaper to keep it warm and help it cook better. It will need to cook for at least an hour to absorb all the liquids in the bag. When it is finished cooking tear the bag down the seam and it will stay in the shape of the bag to look just like a food brick. I loved to put my own honey mustard on the top of it when it was finished. To make the honey mustard all you need is two packs each of mayonnaise, mustard, and sugar. Mix all together and it is done and can be used on anything from your chicken sandwiches and salads to bricks.

No bake cookies are easy to make as well. You will need a pack of regular oatmeal, a pack of peanut butter, a packet of hot coco mix, and a bowl to mix everything into. Add all the ingredients together and if it still does not look quite like the cookies yet add just a spoon full of water to the mix until it looks like the homemade cookie mix, use the lid to the bowl as a tray and spoon the mix into balls and allow to dry on the trays until they make cookies. It usually takes about an hour or so to have them set up and looks like the homemade no bake cookies.

If you have never had a candy bar in your cup of coffee or even put in some hot coco mix, you are really missing out. The best candy bar to use in jail is the three musketeers bar. Run hot water; add the instant coffee mix, and half of a chocolate bar to the cup. Stir until it is foamy and completely dissolved and the coffee looks like a mocha now. It has real chocolate and sugar now in the coffee so now you get your chocolate and caffeine fix in one step.

There are many more things you can fix like egg salad sandwiches or deviled eggs from the boiled eggs we have at breakfast. You can even learn to make brownies and cakes from cookies and candy bars. With enough time you too can come up with better or different ways to cook things inside of jail or prison.

Be Creative

As you soon will find out, everything in jail can be used for more than just one thing. I will tell you about the major items used and reused for things to help make your stay just a little easier on you. I want to let you know right now that most the things I am about to tell you about are against the institution rules and if you do them, you could get into trouble. Every institution is different with different rules and ways they handle things so just keep that in mind, if you decide to use anything I have told you about in this book.

Now I will go into detail about the items that you will find in the indigent kits at the jail and other uses for them. All these items come in a medium sized plastic bag: a small bar of soap, small shampoo bottle, five white folded pieces of paper, five self stamped envelopes, an inmate pen, a small black plastic comb, a small white toothbrush, a small tube of clear toothpaste, and small container of clear deodorant.

The bar of soap looks just like the ones you see inside many hotel rooms. If you have to use it on your body it does not last long. I used it as an air freshener. To do this you can use a clean sock and crush up the soap, and any other little pieces of soap you may have that you do not use anymore, and put it down in the bottom of the sock then tie a knot in the middle of the sock. To use you just shake it around your cell or even beat it against the wall and it will make it smell a lot nicer in there. You can also keep all those little pieces of soap and put them crushed up in an old larger shampoo or conditioner bottle, like Vo5 bottles, run the cell hot water for a long time to get it as hot as you can then add just enough to cover the soap and shake a lot. The soap and water will make a body wash you can use in the shower or even an all-purpose soap to clean your dishes and floors. It is even better if you can add the small bottle of shampoo and any other small amounts of shampoo and conditioner you might have left over. The little bar itself can also be used to remove stains by rubbing it over the area and then use your finger nail to simply scrape it off of your clothes.

The white paper is great to make homemade cards for your friends and family. I will even tell you how you can color the cards and make them smell nice too. First you need to get some Degree deodorant, a sock, and a magazine. Put the sock on your hand rub one finger over the deodorant then over the color you want to use from the magazine. When the color is rubbed on the sock you can now color on the paper. You just repeat the step with the color until you have finished coloring.

The pens you get in jail are very small and flimsy, so they are hard to use well. To fix this problem wrap several pieces of paper around the outside of the pen until it becomes more like a real pen then pull some tape off of the shampoo bottle and tape the paper in place so that it will not unroll. You can even decorate the paper that you use to put around the pen to make it look nice.

The deodorant that comes in the pack is not good to use for hygiene. It is clear and when you sweat it gels up and does not help with smell, in some cases can even make you smell worse. So it is usually used as a heel balm to moisturize your feet. It works very well especially if you put it on your feet after you get out of the shower and then put your socks on. When you get in jail the water will dry out your whole body and can make your feet feel awful. The air quality is so bad on top of the water with all the chemicals in it your hair will fall out for a while too. Some will be worse than others.

Old newspapers can be used to clean windows and the mirrors or all the shiny metal things in the cell. The newspaper leaves everything streak free and very clean.

For women the state issued pads can be used for many things. The biggest thing that they are used for other than the obvious is to clean the common room tables. The metal toilets are very cold to sit on so take a few pads and place them around the toilet seat, sticky side down and now you have a seat warmer and protector. There are vents at the top of each cell and sometimes it will get to hot or cold in your cell and you cannot control the temperature, so place some pads sticky side to the vents to cover up the holes. Some girls will even use those pads to make their own tampons. This can be very dangerous and I will not explain how to do this because if it is done wrong it can cause serious infections. Ear plugs are pretty easy to make but it takes some time to do. Ear plugs are used when people sleep to help keep the noise of the other inmates and sounds of the jail out. To make a sleep mask you can put an unrolled pad in a sock and use a rubber band to tie the ends together then you just slip it over your head to cover your eyes. Pads can also be used as a broom and mop for your cell. They are good to use to clean up any type of spills too.

Make up is a big thing that the girls like to use in jail. To make eyeliner use a pencil and it can be used for eyebrows too. Mascara is made from the indigent clear toothpaste mixed with the ink from a pen, to put it on use a new toothbrush. For lipstick use M&Ms, the color on the outside shells comes off if you wet your lips then run the candy over your lip until the color transfers. You can use the same method for applying eye shadow with the candy too.

Girls can use strips of newspaper rolled up to look like curlers to use in their hair. The hair needs to be damp and then roll the hair around the newspaper rollers and then the hair has to dry. When the hair dries and you take out the rollers it makes very pretty curls.

Men and women both use hair gel sometimes and it is very expensive to buy from jail. It is simple to make and a little can go a long way. You will need the apple jelly packets that come on some of the breakfast trays, a little conditioner, and a container to store it in for future use. Mix several packets of the apple jelly together with the conditioner. If you want it to be extra stiff you can even add a tube of the indigent toothpaste to your homemade hair gel. Make sure everything is mixed well and it is ready to be used. If you use this during the summer ants can be bad and if you leave it in your hair and go to sleep you might wake up with ants in your hair and they are hard to wash out.

You would be surprised at the things that inmates can come up with when you go to jail. Some other things that I have seen are: toilet paper roses, a guitar made from toilet paper rolls, rings made from black trash bags, bracelets made from old torn t-shirts, head bands made from the elastic of underwear, and many other creative things.

Release Day

As the day approaches that you get to leave the institution for good, you will see that many things will now get on your last nerve. Some people even request to be put in maximum security for the last month of their stay. If you have good time that means that you get released early and some of the other inmates can even try to get you into trouble so that you lose that good time. If you get into trouble and get sent to max, when they do your sentencing they have the power to take away your good time that you earned and make you serve out the full sentence the judge gave you. So my best advice would be stay to yourself and if you see that people are going to try and give you a problem, you might want to ask to be moved to max. In my opinion I would rather sit a week or two in max and still be able to leave early than get set up and sent to max and have to stay in jail another month or more because of someone else.

When you walked into jail you will have this feeling that your world has truly came to an end. But when you get ready to leave you will feel like a kid on Christmas morning. You have been locked up with no sunlight for maybe months or longer now and no fresh air! When you walk out of those front doors of the jail you will truly think that you might pass out from the feeling you get. You will notice smells that you never noticed before and see things in a brand new way. The world will seem like it is bigger than ever and I promise you will love the new way you feel about life in general. Things that you use to take for granted like the feel of a warm summer breeze or rain drops, will now feel totally different and amazing. The first time you ride in a car you will most likely get car sick from all the motion. You will get a buzz from your first drink of caffeinated soda. Some people even cry when they leave because you will meet a few good people while in there and will hate to leave them behind. Your first day and last day will feel totally different.

If you are a convicted felon now before you can be released you have to have your DNA sent off to be placed on file. They have to have your DNA, finger prints, and a home plan. A home plan is just what it sounds like, your plan when you get released from your institution on where you will live, work, and function in society. All this must be done before the day you are to be released. They will not let you leave the facility if these things have not been done.

The day you get released they will walk you and all the things that you want to take with you out back to booking where you came in on your first day. When you get there they will run your name to make sure that no other institutions in any states have warrants or holds for you. Once your name is clear they will give you the clothes that you came in with and allow you to change back into your street clothes. When they see that everything is in order, like your correct release date. You will be walked out by an officer with any other inmates to be released and you are free to leave and hopefully never return.

If you have supervised probation you will have anywhere from hours to no more than two days to report to your probation officer. If you do not report they can issue a warrant for your arrest and back to jail you will go when they catch you. Best thing to do is go straight from release to the probation officer anyway just to get it over with and start any community service that the court might have ordered you to do.

You will find out that it is not as bad as you might have once thought. It was a long road but now it is behind you and you can move on with your life and learn from the mistakes that you made that got you to that point. I hope that this book gave you and your loved ones a little comfort when you had to be incarcerated and it is something that you can pass on to others now facing the same long road you just came down.

www.ingramcontent.com/pod-product-compliance
Lightning Source LLC
Chambersburg PA
CBHW021443170526
45164CB00001B/376